I am pleased to write a foreword for this excellent book. Though this book is all about economics but this book is handy for all those who want to pursue their business in the field of Economics. In this book we have focused on all important topics in great details which wil;l give you proper understanding on different topics on Economics. By introducing this book we want to ensure that our readers will be fascinated with the subject and will have good feeling about Economics.

Economics is considerted as boring subjects for those who study in science field. But trust me even though I am from science back ground still I find it very interesting to research new things in Economics. I am fascinated with thr fact that economics can be applied in various feilds and this can save a lot of time, efforts and money.

I wrote this book with one of my collegue named SUHAIL HAQUE who is and indiogenous researcher in Economics. We studied on different Economics topic and wanted to share with opther. So decided to put everything in printable format so that it bvecomes useful to all other persons who love Economics as a subject.

In this book we have defined several important topics that are often asked in various competitive exam papers that has economics as a subject. This book will help you for quick revision and preparing notes for yoru examination.

Thank You!

Vipul Baibhav

(Author)

SUHAIL HAQUE

(Co Author)

Contents

Foreword

People have a misconception that Ecomics can only be understood with those who have economics back ground. In order to eliminate this misconception I started researching on different topics of econimics each day. It is rightly said that human can do whatever they can if they focus on their work with deligency. The result of my tremendous efforts, reading various ebooks, economics jouranals, newspapers resulted in better and closer looks on the economics.

I studied several hours on various topics on economics to understand the various concepts. Although I am not from Economics back ground I put my 100% efforts to produce the book in easiest possible ways. For this I also took help from SUHAIL HAQUE my friend who is from Economics back ground who gave me the topics that are really important in Economics subject. Academic people can be benfited in multiple ways. teachers cna use thios book as a handbook for teaching purposes. It consits of toipics from both ICSE and CBSE curriculum.

"Economics made simple" as the name suggest si benefitial for those who are preparing themselves for competitive examination as well. This short book will cover up entire important topics of economics and give you proper undertsanding of Economics. Using this book we can also preach stuidents in vcollege, universties, as the book reference. The topics are often asked in various examination from time to time.

Preface

I am pleased to write a preface for this excellent book. Though this book is all about economics but this book is handy for all those who want to pursue their business in the field of Economics. In this book we have focused on all important topics in great details which wil;l give you proper understanding on different topics on Economics. By introducing this book we want to ensure that our readers will be fascinated with the subject and will have good feeling about Economics.

Economics is considerted as boring subjects for those who study in science field. But trust me even though I am from science back ground still I find it very interesting to research new things in Economics. I am fascinated with thr fact that economics can be applied in various feilds and this can save a lot of time, efforts and money.

I wrote this book with one of my collegue named SUHAIL HAQUE who is and indiogenous researcher in Economics. We studied on different Economics topic and wanted to share with opther. So decided to put everything in printable format so that it bvecomes useful to all other persons who love Economics as a subject.

In this book we have defined several important topics that are often asked in various competitive exam papers that has economics as a subject. This book will help you for quick revision and preparing notes for yoru examination.

Thank You!

Vipul Baibhav

(Author)

SUHAIL HAQUE

(Co Author)

Acknowledgements

First of all I would like to thank all our readers who took purchased this book and encouraged us to produce amazing books every month. It takes me several hours to research on topics and write it on my own words. I would also like to thank SUHAIL HAQUE who helped me in finsihing this book in quick time. Without his help this book would not have been completed.

No book is successful if we donot give credits to the original researcher who spend their whole life in producing awsome therory in Economics.If you have any further clarification required on any topics you can also send me email and will respond you as soon as possible.

Thanks and Regards
Vipul Baibhav(Author)
(infrasoftltd@gmail.com)
SUHAIL HAQUE(Co-Author)
(suhail_haque@yahoo.com, hi2suhail@gmail.com)

Prologue

Economics is considered to be a difficult subject. People think that Economics is so vast that we cannot revise all the topics during examination time. That is why we have produiced this book in such a way that you will not miss any topic that might come to your examination paper.

Through this book you will get proper understanding of different economic terms, definations and can differentiate them accordingly.We have introduced unique concept for proper undertstanding of various types of Economiy in ngeneral. Not only this we have also outlined the central problems of Economy as well.

Later on we have introduced National income, Classification of countries on the basis of national income, its concept, and methods to measure national income. We also have focused on money its primary function as well as its secondary function.

Then we have defined demands, and its difference with desire, factors affecting demands, types of demand,and its laws. We have also touched various important topics of Supply, factors that affects supply, types of supply, laws of supply and its exceptions, Price elasticity.

Then we have introduced Budget and taxes,its objectives, and importance of budget.After that we have introduced the Five years Plan in Economy. here we have outlined different types of planning, features of planning, and Objective of Indian planning as case study.

At last we have mentioned the success and failure of the planning.

CHAPTER ONE

What is Economics?

Economics is a social science concerned with the production, distribution, and consumption of goods and services. Economics is not just about money. It is about weighing different choices or alternatives. It is the study of how humans make decisions in the face of scarcity. The term "Economics" comes from the Greek word 'oikos' meaning house and 'nomus' meaning customs or law. Therefore, the meaning stands 'Rules of the Household'.

Economics can generally be broken down into 2 categories; macroeconomics and microeconomics. On one hand, Macroeconomics concentrates on the behavior of the economy as a whole, whereas microeconomics, which focuses on individual people and businesses.

What is Macroeconomics?

Macroeconomics studies the economy as a whole, such as national income, aggregate employment, general price level, aggregate consumption, aggregate investment, etc.

The main instruments are aggregate demand and aggregate supply. Macroeconomics is also called the 'Income Theory' or 'Employment Theory'.

There are 3 main macroeconomic goals: economic growth, full employment, and price stability.

Macro economics helps us to understand the functioning of a complicated modern economic system. It describes how the economy as a whole functions and how the level of national income and employment is determined on the basis of aggregate demand and aggregate supply.

What is Microeconomics?

Microeconomics is a branch of economics that studies the behavior of individuals and firms in making decisions regarding the allocation of scarce resources and the interactions among these individuals and firms.

Microeconomics is all about how individual actors make decisions regarding the allocation of resources. In a nutshell, microeconomics has to do with supply and demand, and with the way they interact in various markets.

The theory of micro economics revolves around Consumer demand, Cost-of-production theory of value, Opportunity cost, Price Theory, Markets and finally Supply and demand.

Reasons to Study Economics

There are 3 primary reasons as to why one should study economics;

Variety of programs: economics are part of most aspects of everyday life.

A focus on real life: economics is focused on learning from case studies.

Excellent graduate prospects: most students easily find a job after graduation as economists are needed in most businesses.

More broadly, a degree in Economics will help you to prepare for careers that require numerical, analytical and problem solving skills. Economics helps you to think strategically and make decisions to optimize the outcome.

Economic Problem – An Insightful Guide

An economy is a system by which people set a living. It is also defined as the framework in which entire economic activity takes place.

Ownership of an Economy

Nature of an Economy

Capitalist Economy

Capitalist economy is that economy where the resource of the economy is totally controlled by the private sector. Here, the price is determined by the price mechanism or market mechanism.

Closed Economy

Closed economy is such an economy where international trade does not take place.

Socialist Economy

Socialist economy is that economy where the resource is totally controlled by public sector. The system is put to use under a centralized plan. Here, the price is determined by the government planning only.

Open Economy

Open economy is the framework where export and import take place.

Mixed Economy

Mixed economy is that economy where the resource is simultaneously controlled by the private and public sector. In a mixed economy, some important production is undertaken by the state and some is left for private enterprises. Here the price is determined by both price mechanism and planning.

Planned Economy

In a planned economy, through the centralized plan resources are utilized to its maximum extent.

Complex Economy

It is an economy where science and technology is developed and money is considered as the medium of exchange.

Economic problem is a problem of choice involving satisfaction of unlimited wants out of limited resources having alternative uses.

Economic problem arises because of scarcity of resources in terms of;

1. **Wants are unlimited**

   a. This is a basic fact of human life.
   b. Human wants are unlimited.

c. They are not only unlimited but also grow and multiply very fast.

2. Resources are limited

a. The resources to produce goods and services to satisfy human wants are available in limited quantities. Land, labour, capital and enterprise are the basic scarce resources.
b. These resources are available in limited quantities in every economy, big or small, developed or underdeveloped, rich or poor. Some economies may have more of one or two resources but not all the resources.

3. Resources have alternative uses

a. Generally a resource has many alternative uses.
b. A worker can be employed in a factory, in a school, in a government office, self employed and so on.
c. Nearly all resources have alternative uses, but we need to ensure when to use which resource.

Central Problems of an Economy

The problem of making a choice among alternative uses of resources is known as basic or central problem of an economy.

Every economy has limited resources which can alternatively be used to produce different goods and services. Hence, it has to allocate its available resources in the production of different goods and services in such a manner that it ideally meets the needs of the society.

While allocating resources optimally, the decisions the following three central problems of an economy are required to be taken:

1. What to produce?
2. How to produce?
3. For whom to produce?

In the upcoming section we will understand in details about these 3 central problems of an economy;

1. What to Produce

a. What to produce refers to a problem in which decision regarding which goods and services should be produced is to be taken.

b. Since the resources are limited, every economy has to decide what commodities are to be produced and also in what quantities.

c. In view of limited resources when we produce more of a commodity, it means we will be able to produce less of another. Because more production of one commodity would force us to withdraw resources from the production of the other commodity.

d. So, the economy has to choose between capital goods (like machines, tools, etc.), civil goods (like cloth, watch, radio etc.), consumer goods (like wheat, cloth, shoes, sugar, etc.), military goods (like guns, bombs, tanks, etc.) necessities of life (such as food, clothing, housing, etc.) and luxury goods (such as car, laptops, TV, etc).

e. The guiding principle for an economy here is to allocate resources in such a way that gives maximum aggregate utility to the society.

2. How to Produce

a. How to produce refers to a problem in which decision regarding which technique of production should be used is taken.

b. Goods and services can be produced in two ways: by using labour intensive techniques, and by using capital-intensive techniques.

c. Under labour intensive techniques, more of labour and less of capital per unit of output is used in producing goods and services, while in capital-intensive techniques more of capital and less of labour per unit of output is used.

d. Thus, the economy has to decide whether the chosen goods and services should be produced with the help of automatic machines or handicrafts. Every method of production has its own advantages and disadvantages.

e. For example, on one side use of more capital; i.e., automatic machines, increases the quantity and improves the quality of production but it results in unemployment as it requires lesser number of laborers. On the other side, handicrafts generate more employment but produce smaller amount of production.

f. The guiding principle for an economy in such a case is to decide about the techniques of production on the basis of cost of production. Those techniques of production should be used which lead to the least possible cost per unit of commodity or service.

3. **For Whom to Produce**

a. For whom to produce refers to a problem in which decision regarding which category of people are going to consume a good, i.e., economically poor or rich.
b. As we know, goods and services are produced for those who can purchase them or have the capacity to buy them.
c. Capacity to buy depends upon how income is distributed among the factors of production. The higher the income, the higher will be the capacity to buy and vice Versa. So, this is a problem of distribution.
d. We know that the whole output is distributed among factors of production which have contributed to it.
e. Since production is the combined efforts of all the four factors of production, viz, land, labour, capital and enterprise, it is distributed among them in the form of money income (i.e. rent, wages, interest and profits). Who should get how much is, thus, the problem.
f. The guiding principle is that the economy must see here that important and urgent wants of its citizens are being satisfied to the maximum possible extent or not.

Points to Ponder On

Father of Economics

Adam Smith was an 18th-century Scottish economist, philosopher, and author, who lived from 1723 to 1790, is considered the father and founder of modern economics. Smith is most famous for his 1776 book, "The Wealth of Nations."

Mother of Economics

Amartya Sen has been called the Mother Teresa of Economics for his work on famine, human development, welfare economics, and the underlying mechanisms of poverty, gender inequality, and political liberalism.

CHAPTER TWO

National Income

The national income of a nation is nothing but the sum total of factors income for a particular time period. According to the National Income Committee of India, "A national income estimate measurers the volume of commodities and services turned out during a given period counted without duplication."

Thus, national income measures the flow of goods and services in an economy. National income is a flow and not a stock concept. In India, national income estimates are related with the financial year – i.e. from 1stApril of the current year to the 31stMarch of the next year.

Classification of Economy in terms of National Income

According to the growth of National Income, an economy can be classified into;

Developed Economy

Developed Economy is that economy where per capita income is evry high as well as the standard of living is very high.

Under Developed Economy

Under Developed Economy is that economy where the growth rate of national income and the per capita income is very less than that of optimum level.

Developing Economy

Developing Economy is that economy where the per capita income is rising.

Concepts of National Income

The different concepts of the national income have been discussed below;

Gross National Product (GNP)

Gross National Product refers to the money value of all final goods and services produced by the nationals of a country during a given period of time, generally a year. Part of the GNP is earned from abroad.

Gross Domestic Product (GDP)

Gross Domestic Product is the value of all final goods and services produced within a country for a given time period, generally a year.

GNP is equal to $GDP + X - M$ where

X determines the income earned and received by the citizen from foreign countries whereas M determines the income received by foreign nationals from domestic country.

Net National Product (NNP)

Net National Product is obtained by subtracting depreciation value (i.e. capital stock consumption) from GNP.

Thus, NNP = GNP − Depreciation

National Income

Net National Product can be calculated in 2 ways;

1. at market price of goods and services
2. at factor cost

Goods valued without net indirect taxes (i.e. total indirect taxes - subsidy) is known as factor cost valuation when Net National Product (NNP) is calculated at factor cost, it is known as National Income.

Thus, Net National Product at factor cost implies;

= NNP at market price − Net indirect tax

= NNP at market price − (Indirect taxes - Subsidy)

= NNP at market price − (Indirect taxes + Subsidy)

Personal Income

Personal Income is an income which is actually obtained by nationals. It refers to the income received by the individuals of a country in a year from all sources. Thus, personal income is a flow concept.

Personal Disposal Income

Personal Disposal Income (PDI) can be defined in 2 ways;

1. PDI = Personal Income − Personal Direct Tax Payment
2. PDI = Personal Consumption + Personal Savings

Corporate Income

Corporate Income means income and profits of companies or public corporation. If income tax and profit tax is deducted, then corporate income is derived.

Per Capita Income

Per Capita Income of a country may be defined as average earning of an individual in a particular year. Per capita income or PCI can be defined as;

PCI = Total National Income / Total Population

Methods of Measuring National Income

According to Kuznets, national income of a country can be calculated by the following methods;

Product Method or Output Method

Here the net value of final goods and services produced in a country during a year is calculated.

To avoid multiple counting, only the final value of goods and services are considered.

Income Method

Income method focuses on finding the total output of a nation by finding the total income of a nation. National income is obtained by adding the receipts as total rent, total wages, total interest and total profit.

Expenditure Method or Consumption Method

Income of an individual is either spent on the consumption or saved. Thus, the calculation of national income is determined by adding the total consumption and total savings.

CHAPTER THREE

Money

In the primitive times, the concept was money was not fully relevant. People were more convenient using a very unique system known as the "Barter", where they used to transact using goods.

Although, it was difficult to understand the exact value, but it was the order of the day. For example; wheat may be exchanged for cloth; house for horses, etc., or a teacher may be paid wheat or rice as a payment for his/her services.

Barter as a system of exchange had its own set of difficulties;

1. Barter is possible only if goods produced by two persons are needed by each other. It is double coincidence of wants. Here *"Double coincidence of wants"* means that the goods in possession of the 2 different persons must be useful and should be needed by each other. This is the main basis of barter system of exchange. But it is rare. Not all the time, both the person might require those 2 things.

2. In commodity exchange, barter system will pose a serious threat and the difficulty of dividing the commodity is sure to arise.

3. It is very difficult to store wealth for future use. Most of the goods like wheat, rice, cattle etc. are likely to deteriorate with the passage of time or involve heavy cost of storage.

4. Transfer of immovable commodities (such as house, farm, land, etc.) becomes almost impossible.

5. Different commodities are of different values. The value of a good or service means the amount of other goods and services it can be exchanged for in the market. There is no common measure of value under barter system.

6. There could be disagreement regarding the quality of the goods or services to be repaid.

Later, money was introduced as a standard medium of exchange. It can be classified into 4 categories of 2 main functions;

1. Primary Function

The primary function of money includes the most important functions that must be performed in an economic system irrespective of time and place.

- **Medium of Exchange**

Money when used as a medium of exchange helps in the elimination of the basic limitation of barter trade, and eases of the lack of double coincidence of wants. Thus, the process of exchange shall have two parts: a sale and a purchase.

- **Measure of Value**

Another important function of money is that it serves as a common measure of value or a unit of account. Money acts as a common denominator into which the values of all goods and services are expressed.

2. Secondary Function

Money means classified as both goods and services. The secondary functions encompass money as a standard of deferred payments as well as a store for value.

- **Standard of Deferred Payment**

Credit has become the life and blood of a modern capitalist economy. In the present day business scenario, instant payments are not made. The debtors make a promise that they will make payments on some future date.

- **Store of Value**

Wealth can be conveniently stored in the form of money. Money can be stored without loss in value. Savings are secured and can be used whenever

there is a need thereby acting as a bridge between the present and the
future.

CHAPTER FOUR

Demand

Demandis a quantity of a commodity which a consumer wishes to purchase at a given level of price and during a specified period of time.

In other words, demand for a commodity refers to the desire to buy a commodity backed with sufficient purchasing power and the willingness to spend.

How is Demand different from that of Desire?

Desireis just a wish for a commodity and a person can desire a commodity even if he does not have the capacity to buy it from the market whereas demand is desire backed by purchasing power that is to say whatever an individual is willing to buy from the market in a given period of time at a given price. A poor person can desire to own a car but that will not become a demand because he does not have the purchasing power to buy a car from the market.

Factors affecting personal (individual) demand

Individual demand function refers to the functional relationship between individual demand and the factors affecting the individual demand. Here are some of the crucial factors that can affect an individual in a numerous ways;

- Price of the commodity
- Price of related goods

  - Substitute Goods
  - Complementary Goods

- ○ Income of a Consumer

- Taste and Preferences of the Consumer

Factors affecting the Market demand:

Market demand refers to the quantity of a commodity that all the consumers are willing and able to buy, at a particular price during a given period of time. Here are some of the crucial factors that can affect the market in numerous ways;

- Price of the commodity
- Price of related commodity
- Income of a consumer
- Taste and preference of a consumer
- Miscellaneous
- Population Size
- Distribution of Income

Causes of Law of Demand and Exceptions to Law of Demand

Causes of Law of Demand

- Quantity demanded of a commodity changes due to change in purchasing power (real income), caused by change in price of a commodity is called Income Effect.
- Any change in the price of a commodity affects the purchasing power or real income of consumers although his money income remains the same.
- When price of a commodity rises more has to be spent on purchase of the same quantity of that commodity. Thus, rise in price of commodity leads to fall in real income, which will thereby reduce quantity demanded is known as **Income effect.**
- It refers to substitution of one commodity in place of another commodity when it becomes relatively cheaper.
- A rise in price of the commodity let coke, also means that price of its substitute, let PEPSI, has fallen in relation to that of coke, even though

the price of PEPSI remains unchanged. So, people will buy more of PEPSI and less of coke when price of coke rises. In other words, consumers will substitute PEPSI for coke. This is called **Substitution effect.**

- **Law of Diminishing Marginal Utility**states that when a consumer consumes more and more units of a commodity, every additional unit of a commodity gives lesser and lesser satisfaction and marginal utility decreases.
- Old consumers of the commodity start demanding more of the same commodity by spending the same amount of money. As the result, of the old and the new buyers push up the demand for a commodity when price falls.

Exceptions to the of Law of Demand

- Giffen goods are a special category of inferior goods in which demand for a commodity falls with a fall in its price.
- In case of certain inferior goods when their prices fall, their demand may not rise because extra purchasing power (caused by fall in prices) is diverted on purchase of superior goods.
- These goods are purchased by the household in increased quantities even when their prices are rising upwards.
- Status symbol goods are purchased not because of their intrinsic value but because of status or prestige value.

Aggregate Demand

Aggregate demand refers to the total demand for final goods and services in an economy during an accounting year. Aggregate demand is aggregate expenditure on ex-ante (planned) consumption and ex-ante (planned) investment that all sectors of the economy are willing to incur at each income level.

Components of aggregate demand:

The 2 components of aggregate demand are:

- Private (or Household) consumption demand

The total expenditure incurred by all the households of the country on their personal consumption is known as private consumption expenditure.

- Private investment demand

Private investment demand refers to the demand for capital goods by private investors.

CHAPTER FIVE

Supply

Supply refers to the quantity of a commodity that a firm is willing and able to offer for sale, at each possible price during a given period of time. In other words, supply is that part of stock which is actually brought into the market for sale. Stock can never be less than supply.

Stock refers to total quantity of a particular commodity that is available with the firm at a particular point of time.

Market supply refers to the quantity of a commodity that all firms are willing and able to offer for sale at each possible price during a given period of time.

Factors affecting personal (individual) supply:

Here are some of the crucial factors that can affect an individual in a numerous ways;

- Price of the commodity
- Price of the factors of production
- State of technology
- Unit tax
- Price of other goods
- Objective of the firm

Factors affecting Market supply:

Here are some of the crucial factors that can affect a market in a numerous ways;

- Price of the commodity
- Price of the factors of production
- State of technology
- Unit tax
- Price of other goods
- Objective of the firm
- Number of firms in the market
- Future Expectation regarding price

Causes to the Law of Supply

- There is a positive relationship between price of the commodity and quantity supplied for that commodity which causes supply curve to slope upward from left to right.
- With the increase in the price of the commodity sellers are ready to sell more from their old stock of goods.
- On the other hand, when price of a commodity decreases, sellers would like to increase their stock to avoid losses.
- With the rise in price producers, they increase their production in view of higher profit possibilities and vice-versa.
- When the price of a commodity increases, new firms enter into the industry with the view to earn profits which in turn increases the supply.
- On the other hand, when price starts falling, marginal firms (or inefficient firms) leave the market to avoid expected losses which thereby decreases the supply.

Exceptions to the Law of Supply

- The law will not apply if there are future expectations for further change in prices.
- The supply of agricultural goods depends more on natural factors such as drought, floods, natural calamities etc. and less on their prices.
- The supply of perishable goods, like milk, vegetables, fish, eggs, etc. is also not affected by their prices. Sellers cannot hold these goods for long.

- Artistic goods of high quality and poems written by top class poets come under this category. Their supply cannot be increased even when their prices rise.
- The law of supply loses its applicability in backward countries where the production and supply cannot be increased merely because of rise in prices.

Factors Affecting Price Elasticity of Supply

- Nature of the commodity
- Cost of production
- Time period
- Technique of production
- Availability of the resources and facilities

Aggregate Supply

The concept of aggregate supply (ΔS) is related with the total supply of goods and services by all the producers in an economy. Four factor of production like land, labour, capital and enterprise are required for the production of goods and services.

Producers pay rent to land, wages and salaries to labour, interest to capital and Profits to the entrepreneur for their services in production. This payment is factor- cost from producer's point of view and factor-income from factor-owner angle.

Thus, aggregate supply is the total amount of money value of goods and services, (which is paid to the factor of production against their factor services) that all the producers are willing to supply in an economy. In other words, it is the total cost of production of goods and services produced in a country or it is the value of net national product at factor cost (NNPFC).

Components of aggregate supply:
The main components of aggregate supply are:

- Wages
- Rent

- ◦ Interest
- ◦ Profit

CHAPTER SIX

Budget & Taxes

A government budget is an annual financial statement showing item wise estimates of expected revenue and anticipated expenditure during a fiscal year. Budget is the most important instrument in hands of governments to achieve their objectives and there lies the importance of the government budget.

Budgets consist of 2 parts;

1. Receipts; and
2. Expenditure

Objectives of the Budget

Here are so

- Private enterprises always desire to allocate resources to those areas of production where profits are high.
- (However, it is possible that such areas of production (like production of alcohol) may not promote social welfare.
- Through its budgetary policy the government of a country directs the allocation of resources in a manner such that there is a balance between the goals of profit maximization and social welfare.
- Production of goods which are injurious to health (like cigarettes and whisky) is discouraged through heavy taxation.
- Budget of a government shows its comprehensive exercise on the taxation and subsidies.
- A government uses fiscal instruments of taxation and subsidies with a view of improving the distribution of income and wealth in the

economy.

- A government reduces the inequality in the distribution of income and wealth by imposing taxes on the rich and giving subsidies to the poor, or spending more on welfare of the poor.
- It reduces income of the rich and raises the living standard of the poor, thus, leads to equitable distribution of income.
- Expenditure on special anti poverty and employment schemes will be increased to bring more people above poverty line.
- Public distribution system should be inferred so that only the poor could get food grains and other essential items at subsidized prices.
- Free play of market forces (or the forces of supply and demand) is bound to generate trade cycles, also called business cycles.
- Economic stability leads to more investment and increases the rate of growth and development.

Importance of a budget

Today every country aims at its economic growth to improve living standard of its people. Besides, there are many other problems such as poverty, unemployment, inequalities in incomes and wealth etc. Government strives hard to solve these problems through budgetary measures.

The budget shows the fiscal policy. Itemwise estimates of expenditure disclose how much and on what items, the government is going to spend. Similarly, item wise details of government receipts indicate the sources from where the government intends to get money to finance the expenditure.

Note: Fiscal year is the year in which country's budgets are prepared. Its duration is from 1st April to 31st March.

Five Year Plan in Indian Economy

Economic planning is a process by which some pre determined and well defined objectives and targets are laid down by a Central Planning Authority in order to solve some socio economic problems through proper utilization of resources of an economy.

Different Types of Planning

1. Physical and Financial Planning
2. Centralized and Decentralized Planning
3. Indicative and Imperative Planning
4. Regional, National and International Planning
5. Structural and Functional Planning
6. Democratic and Totalitarian Planning

Features of Indian Planning

1. India's planning is indicative economic planning – not imperative in nature
2. India's economic planning is almost physical planning
3. India's economic planning is decentralized planning
4. Indian planning is developmental planning
5. Indian planning is social planning rather pure economic planning
6. It is medium term planning

7. It is democratic planning

Objectives of Indian Planning

India's economic planning is basically development oriented planning where the basic aim is to achieve overall economic development of our economy.

The prime objectives of India's economic planning are drawn from the Directive Principles of State Policy of the Indian Constitution (Part - IV). The crucial objectives perused in each plan, have been listed below;

1. Economic growth
2. Social justice and equity
3. Employment generation
4. Poverty eradication
5. Modernization, and
6. Self Reliance

Objectives of the 5 Year Plans in Indian Economy

Objectives of 1ˢᵗ Five Year Plan (1951 - 52 & 1955 - 56)

1. Increase agricultural production

2. Solve the problem of refugees

3. Development of rural infrastructure

4. Targeted growth rate of 2.1% p.a. (actual 3.6% p.a.)

Remarks:-

1. Maximum emphasis was given on agricultural sector

2. National Development Council was set up on Aug. 6, 1952

Objectives of 2ⁿᵈ Five Year Plan (1956 - 57 & 1960 - 61)

1. Achieving industrialization in the long term by emphasizing on heavy and basic industries as mentioned in the Mahalanobis Growth strategy

2. Solving the problem of unemployment

3. Annual growth rate was fixed at 4.5%

Remarks:-

1. Maximum emphasis was given on development of heavy and basic capital goods industries

2. The Mahalanobis Model of Planned development strategy was adopted as a development strategy

3. Most important industries of Durgapur, Rourkella, and Bhillai were established with the assistance of Great Britain, Germany and USSR respectively.

Objectives of 3rd Five Year Plan (1956 - 57 & 1960 - 61)

1. Achieving self-reliance in the economy and attaining self-sufficiency in food grains and raw materials.

2. Achieving self sustaining growth through changes of savings and investment.

3. Targeted growth rate was 5.6% p.a. (Actual 25% p.a.)

Remarks:-

1. Almost equal emphasis was given on agriculture and industry.

2. The first Prime Minister Pt. J. L. Nehru died on 27th May 1964

3. The term "Self Reliance" was mentioned for the first time in this plan period.

Objectives of Plan Holiday (1966 - 67 & 1968 - 69)

Traditionally, the 4thFive Year Plan was proposed to start on April 1966. However, the 4thFive Year Plan did not start in scheduled time due to failure of the 3rdFive Year Plan. Instead of this, 3 Annual Plans were implemented in the 3 consecutive years of 1966 to 1969. This era of annual plans is popularly known as the era of "Plan Holiday".

Remarks:

1. In 1966 – 67, a revolutionary change had taken place in agricultural production. This was known as Green Revolution.
2. On June 1, 1966 Indian Rupee was devalued to increase exports.

Objectives of 4thFive Year Plan (1969 - 70 & 1973 - 74)

1. Maintain "social justice and equity" by improving economic conditions of economically weaker section of society.

2. Achieving 'self reliance' by reducing foreign assistance

3. Compound growth rate was 5.7% p.a. (Actual 3.3% p.a.)

Remarks:-

1. The objective of 'Social Justice and Equity' was mentioned explicitly for the first time in the document of the 4thFive Year Plan

2. The slogan – "Garibi Hatao" was coined in 1971 by Indira Gandhi

3. 14 important commercial banks were nationalized

Objectives of 5thFive Year Plan (1974 - 75 & 1977 - 78)

1. Eradication of poverty

2. Achieving economic self-reliance

3. Growth rate was targeted at an annual rate of 4.37% (revised) (Actual: 4.9% p.a. at 1980 -81 prices)

Remarks:-

1. The 5thFive Year Plan directly attacked on poverty for the first time in India.

2. The plan was terminated on March 31, 1978 along with political changes before one year of its completion.

Rolling Plan in Indian Economy (1978 – 80)

The first Non Congress government at the centre, the Janata Govt. came into power in 1977. They terminated in the 5thFive Year Plan in 1978. The Janata Govt. formulated a drafting of economic planning for 1978 to 1983 – known as the Janata Sixth Plan.

Along with it an annual plan was formulated for 1978 – 79. The drafting of such plan was formulated on the basis on the concept of Rolling Plan propounded by Economist Ragner Frisch.

Objectives of 6thFive Year Plan (1980 - 80 & 1984 - 85)

1. Solving the problems of poverty and unemployment simultaneously

2. To modernize the economy

3. To improve living standard of economically weaker sections of society.

4. The compound growth rate of GDP was fixed at 5.2% p.a. (Actual: 5.4% p.a.).

Remarks:-

1. Objective of Modernization was introduced explicitly in the document of the 6thplan.

2. Various programmes like IRDP, NREP, RLEGP, etc. were introduced in order to solve the problems of poverty and unemployment simultaneously.

3. NABARD was set up on July 12, 1982.

Objectives of 7thFive Year Plan (1985 - 86 & 1989 - 90)

1. Establish self-reliant and independent economic system

2. To maintain self reliance by export promotion and import substitution.

3. The growth rate of GDP was fixed at an annual rate of 5% p.a. (Actual: 5.8% p.a.)

Remarks:-

1. "Operation Blackboard" was introduced in 1987 – 88 in order to develop primary education.

2. Main focus of the 7thFive Year Plan was on "Food, Work and Productivity"

3. Agricultural development led strategy was preferred by the planners as a substitute of development strategy adopted in the earlier phase of our planning era.

Annual Plans (1990 – 91 & 1991 - 92)

During these 2 Annual Plans, our economy was reeling on some severe economic crisis like hyper inflationary pressure, BOP deficits, etc. Also, by the end of the 7thFive Year Plan, some political changes took place in India. As a result of these, no Five Year Plans were formulated.

Remarks:

1. In July 1991, the New Economic Policy of India was published
2. Some structural adjustment programmes adopted along with inception of New Economic Policy in India.

Objectives of 8thFive Year Plan (1992 - 92 & 1996 - 97)

1. To generate adequate employment in order to achieve full employment by 2000

2. To strengthen infrastructure as power, transport and communication system in order to achieve sustainable economic development.

3. Targeted / GDP growth rate was 5.6% p.a. (Actual was 6.8% p.a.)

Remarks:-

1. The 8[th]Five Year Plan is the first post reform era plan.

2. Era of 8[th]Five Year Plan can be treated as "Water Shade Line" in Indian Planning era.

3. The indicative and decentralized features of India's economic planning had been more prominent in the 8[th]plan.

Objectives of 9[th]Five Year Plan (1997 - 98 & 2001 - 02)

1. Priority to agriculture and rural development with a view to generate adequate productive employment and eradication of poverty.

2. Developing people's participatory institutions like Panchayati Raj Institutions, self-help groups.

3. Maintenance of regional balance.

Remarks:-

1. Starting of Sarva Sikhsha Abhiyaan in November 2000

2. Narasimham Committee submitted its second report in 1998, regarding banking sector reforms.

3. Introduction of Pradhan Mantri Gram Sadak Yojana on 25[th]Dec. 2000.

Objectives of 10[th]Five Year Plan (2002 - 03 & 2006 - 07)

1. Ensure equity and social justice in the economy through adoption of certain special programs.

2. Ensuring balanced development in all states.

3. The proposed growth rate of GDP during the era of the 10thFive Year Plan should be 8% p.a. on average.

Remarks:-

1. National Food for Work program was launched in November 14, 2004 in 150 under developed districts.

2. Kelkar Committee submitted its report in November 2002 regarding the tax reform of India.

Objectives of 11thFive Year Plan (2007 - 08 & 2011 - 12)

1. Prepared by the C. Rangarajan, the duration of this economic planning was from 2007 to 2012, under the leadership of Man Mohan Singh.
2. Its main theme was "rapid and more inclusive growth".
3. It achieved a growth rate of 8% against a target of 9% growth.

Here are some of the main focuses of the 11thFive Year Plan;

The main focusof the 11thFive Year Plan suggests "Towards Faster and More Inclusive Growth".

1. Average growth rate of GDP is 9% p.a.
2. Increase agricultural GDP growth rate to A% per year to ensure a broader spread of benefits.
3. Generation of 50 million employment opportunities.
4. Reduction in education unemployment to below 5%
5. Reduce dropout rates of children from elementary school from 52.2% in 2003-04 to 20% by 2011-12
6. Attain WHO standards of air quality in all major cities by 2011-12
7. Increase literary rate for persons of age 7 years or more to 85%

8. Reduce Infant Mortality rate (IMR) to 28 and Maternal Mortality Rate (MMR) to 1 per 100 live births.
9. Reduce malnutrition among children of age group 0 to 3 to half of its present level.

Objectives of 12th Five Year Plan (2012 -17)

1. The duration of the 12th Five Year Plan is from 2012 to 2017, under the leadership of Man Mohan Singh.
2. Its main theme is "Faster, More Inclusive and Sustainable Growth".
3. The growth rate target of the 12th Five Year Plan was 8%.

CHAPTER EIGHT

Overall Success and Failure of India's Economic Planning

Success of Planning

1. Without planning, we possibly could not have a proper base of heavy and basic industry.
2. It draws attention to poverty eradication for balanced development of all sections of the society.
3. It gives importance to curb inflation and ensure a sense of stability in the economy.
4. Planning helps to focus on challenges of containing price rise and requirements of economic growth.
5. Indian economy is becoming more open to the world.

Failure of Planning

1. Due importance is not given to development and growth of service sector.
2. Regional disparity is very high
3. There is absence of dedicated emphasis on poverty eradication
4. There is very little investment or allocation of resources on infrastructure development
5. There is no emphasis on the proper functioning of the delivery system and deviations noticed in its lop sided functioning and all these lead to

implementation failure of India's economic planning.

A Word From Author

At the end would like to thank all our readers for showing interest and encouring us to write expelary books on variopus topics. I would also like to thank Notion Press Publ;ication house for the extra ordinary help in providing excellent platform to publish this book in printable format. I hope this book will help all students, teachers, professors of various colleges and will not let the efforts and hard works of every researchers who took their precious time in researching on topics of Economics in great detail.

If you want to get in touch with the author you cna send us mail or contact our publication house.The book is for those who are looking forward to make their carreer in the field of ecomics and want to be known as reknowned future economists.

We expect you might have enjoyed this book. In case you want to suggest, give your remarks, or send us feedback we would appreciate you and will gladly accept to imporve our work.

Thanks and regards
Vipul Baibhav(Author)
SUHAIL HAQUE(Co-Author)